Color Your Way to a Life You Love

ENCOURAGE YOURSELF

A SELF-HELP ADULT COLORING BOOK FOR RELAXATION & PERSONAL GROWTH!

60 CALMING DESIGNS TO COLOR!
FLOWERS & NATURE
ANIMALS
MANDALAS
DOODLES & PATTERNS

COLOR YOUR WAY TO A LIFE YOU LOVE™: ENCOURAGE YOURSELF

For information:
shellijohnson.com
alphadollmedia.com

Copyright Notice and Disclaimers

This book is Copyright © 2017 Shelli Johnson (the "Author"). All Rights Reserved. Published in the United States of America. The legal notices, disclosures, and disclaimers within this book are copyrighted by the Internet Attorneys Association LLC and licensed for use by the Author in this book. All rights reserved.

No part of this book may be reproduced or transmitted in any form or by any means, electronic or mechanical, including photocopying, recording, or by an information storage and retrieval system -- except by a reviewer who may quote brief passages in a review to be printed in a magazine, newspaper, blog, or website -- without permission in writing from the Author. For information, please contact the Author at the following website address: shellijohnson.com/contact

For more information, please read the "Disclosures and Disclaimers" section at the end of this book.

First Paperback Print Edition, October 2017

Published by Alpha Doll Media, LLC (the "Publisher").

ISBN: 978-0-9747109-2-1

WELCOME TO THE
COLOR YOUR WAY TO A LIFE YOU LOVE™
COLORING BOOK SERIES!

 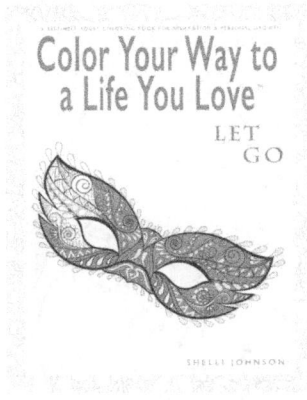 

AVAILABLE NOW OR COMING SOON!

UNLEASH YOUR INNER CREATOR & MAKE IT YOUR OWN!

This is not just another coloring book, it's also an invitation for you to delve deeper into who you are so you can find out what makes you come alive. I'm a big believer in the power of taking small steps to get you anywhere you need or want to go. With that in mind, I invite you inside these pages on a creative self-help adventure. You'll unleash your artistic side with designs and patterns while you do daily small-sized activities aimed at: 1. helping you heal yourself and 2. inspiring you to create a life you love. My hope is that you'll use these pages to ignite your imagination, discard your limitations, and free your inner creator.

Feel free to add your own personal embellishments to any image. You can make each page as unique as you like by adding doodles, patterns, and/or shapes. Color the images any way you like with any tools you like. There are no rules except that you relax, enjoy, and color in a way that feels right to you.

THE MEANING & PURPOSE OF LIFE!

"The meaning of life is to find your gift. The purpose of life is to give it away."
—Pablo Picasso

THE PSYCHOLOGY OF COLOR!

From my layman's understanding of the meaning of colors, certain colors can evoke certain emotions.

BLUE: centered, calm, hopeful, confidence
GREEN: growth, safety, endurance, calm
ORANGE: energy, happiness, encouragement, excitement
RED: passion, energy, strength, power, determination
YELLOW: joy, energy, cheerfulness
BROWN: stability
PURPLE: power, ambition, creativity, energy
BLACK: power, elegance, mystery
WHITE: light, goodness, safety

So keep that in mind as you color. If you're looking to experience a particular emotion/feeling/mood, you may want to use a particular color to help you get there.

A FEW HELPFUL SUGGESTIONS!

BABY STEPS
I'm a big believer in the power of taking baby steps to get you anywhere you need or want to go, which is why this coloring book is written the way it is. Each day has small-sized activities. They build on each other, one to the next. So feel free to color whichever image you'd like, just know you'll be best served to do the daily activities in order.

NO PERFECTION NEEDED
Do yourself a kindness and make a mistake in this coloring book early on. Scribble on some of the pages. Spill your favorite beverage on the cover. Rip one of the corners off. Color outside the lines. Make this book imperfect so that you'll feel free to be your real, honest self inside the pages. Being real, not being perfect, is what's going to heal you and set you free.

BE HONEST
I'd recommend that you don't show your answers inside this coloring book to anyone. Keep them to yourself for right now until you make it all the way through Day 30. Why? Honesty with yourself is what's going to help you heal and grow. You won't be completely honest if you're worried about someone reading your answers. In fact, what you're likely to do is tweak your responses, edit them, or scratch them out entirely if you're worried about how others might perceive you. So be kind to yourself & let this coloring book be just for you.

BE WILLING & OPEN
The first step to change is to be open & willing to it. You picked up this coloring book because you're struggling in this area of your life. If you want things to be different, well, both you & those things are going to have to change. So be open to experiencing something new & be willing to do the effort to get there.

GIVE YOURSELF PERMISSION
It's hugely important to give yourself permission (whether that's verbally or written) to: do the daily steps in this book, be/have/do/say/believe whatever you need to so that you can heal yourself, give yourself unlimited tries as many times as it takes, believe in your own worth and value, choose to create a life you love because you matter. Whenever you feel like you need someone else's permission to make a choice about your life, you just give that permission to yourself. The only permission you ever need to live your own life is your own.

YOU'RE ON A JOURNEY
It doesn't matter how old you are, how many times you've tried, or how far there is left to go. It's never too late to be the person you want to be. It's okay if you don't know things yet. You're on a journey and you'll figure it out as you go. This coloring book is designed to help you do just that.

BEGIN YOUR DAY WITH A STEP
If at all possible, do your daily step shortly after you wake up. That way, you'll be able to focus on yourself (because you're absolutely worth the time to do that) before your day gets away from you. So grab your favorite beverage. Find a quiet place. Relax and reflect while you're being creative.

IT'S A PRACTICE & A PROCESS
There's no doing this perfectly, and that's okay. You strive for progress. You do the best you can. So show yourself some patience and kindness because self-compassion is what you most need to heal yourself. You will make mistakes, there's just no way around it. Don't ever use any mistake as a reason to give up on yourself. Just circle back around and start again. And know this: every mistake is simply a brand new chance to do it better the next time.

AND FINALLY . . .
Remember (not just for this book but for all of life): you get out what you put in. So make yourself a priority in your own life because: 1. you're absolutely worth the effort and 2. no one else can do it for you. And one last suggestion good both for this book and for all of life: be brave and color outside the lines, that's where freedom lies.

THOSE WHO ARE BRAVE ARE FREE!

"It is not the critic who counts; not the man who points out how the strong man stumbles, or where the doer of deeds could have done them better. The credit belongs to the man who is actually in the arena, whose face is marred by dust and sweat and blood; who strives valiantly; who errs, who comes short again and again, because there is no effort without error and shortcoming; but who does actually strive to do the deeds; who knows great enthusiasms, the great devotions; who spends himself in a worthy cause; who at the best knows in the end the triumph of high achievement, and who at the worst, if he fails, at least fails while daring greatly, so that his place shall never be with those cold and timid souls who neither know victory nor defeat."

—Theodore Roosevelt

Source: excerpt (also known as *The Man In The Arena*) from the speech "Citizenship in a Republic" delivered at The Sorbonne in Paris, France on April 23, 1910.

COLOR TEST PAGE

They tried to bury us. They did not know we were seeds.
—Mexican Proverb

1

1. Today, relax.
2. Take a deep breath in through your nose.
3. Hold it for three seconds.
4. Let it out through your mouth.
5. Then pull your shoulders down away from your ears.
6. Repeat five times.
7. Massage your temples & the back of your neck.
8. Repeat often, especially every time you feel discouraged & you need to refocus.

2

1. Today, know that you are not alone.
2. You may feel alone. You may feel like nobody has ever felt as discouraged as you do right now.
3. But know this: I have been there. So have most (if not all) of the people around you. You're likely comparing your insides to other people's outsides (which is a cruel act of self-violence).
4. So don't be so hard on yourself. Instead, remind yourself that you're not alone, that you are in fact in excellent company with the rest of us who've been discouraged, as often as needed.

3

1. Today, speak strength to yourself.
2. Find some favorite quotes or make up your own. Anything that makes you feel stronger & more capable. Write them down.
3. Tack them up where you'll see them.
4. Read them aloud. Even better, look in a mirror while you're doing it. Repeat often.
5. Know this: you'll be victorious or defeated by what you say about yourself.

4

1. Today, remind yourself just how spectacular you really are.
2. Write down at least five positive attributes that you admire or appreciate about yourself.
3. Read that list aloud slowly & let each one sink in. Believe them.
4. Notice how your body feels afterward (energized? happy? free?).
5. Add at least one positive self-attribute to that list *every day*.
6. Read that list whenever you need a reminder that you're awesome as-is.

Look in the mirror. Smile. Tell yourself words you really need to hear.

5

1. Today, change how you talk about yourself.
2. Remember from Day 3: you'll be victorious or defeated by what you say about yourself.
3. So don't say anything negative about yourself to you or to anyone else.
4. If you do, notice how your body feels (defeated? tired? sad? weak?) then *gently* remind yourself to stop.
5. Look at your list from Day 4. Add one more positive self-attribute.
6. Then tell yourself something positive instead.

Look in the mirror. Smile. Tell yourself words you really need to hear.

1. Today, change what you think about yourself.
2. Know this: you are exactly what you think you are.
3. So don't think anything negative about yourself.
4. If you do, notice how your body feels (defeated? tired? sad? weak?) then *gently* reject that thought. (Yes, you can reject any thought you choose to.)
5. Look at your list from Day 4. Add one more positive self-attribute. Then think one or more of those things about yourself instead.

Look in the mirror. Smile. Tell yourself words you really need to hear.

7

1. Today, let loose for a little while.
2. Watch/read something funny. Or goof around with someone. Or play with your pet. Do whatever you like that makes you laugh. (This is especially important if you don't much feel like laughing.)
3. Know this: it's all going to be okay (yes, in the end it will be). So let yourself belly laugh at some point today.
4. Repeat often.
5. Reminder: add one more positive self-attribute to your list from Day 4.

Look in the mirror. Smile. Tell yourself words you really need to hear.

8

1. Today, make a personal mantra.
2. Write down three positive words that you want to live your life by.
3. Make a mantra out of them: I am [fill in your three words].
4. Say that mantra out loud. Repeat often.
5. Those words are your strong foundation. Now build your life on top of them.
6. Come back to that short phrase whenever you find yourself discouraged or being negative.

Look in the mirror. Smile. Tell yourself words you really need to hear.

1. Today, move more.
2. Write a list of exercises you like to do, *anything* that gets you moving.
3. Know this: the best exercise for you is the one you'll do.
4. Now pick one & go do it. Repeat *daily*.
5. Know this too: doing some kind of exercise that gets you moving releases feel-good biochemicals in your brain. Exercise is a natural way to feel better about yourself & your life, which will encourage you.
6. Reminder: add one more positive self-attribute to your list from Day 4.

Look in the mirror. Smile. Tell yourself words you really need to hear.

10

1. Today, love where you live.
2. Create a relaxing space in your home, somewhere tailored just for you.
3. Fill it with your favorite things.
4. Go there sometime today for at least fifteen minutes.
5. During that time, close your eyes then take ten deep breaths (in through your nose, hold three seconds, then let it out your mouth).
6. Repeat often.
7. Go to that space whenever you need a little pick-me-up.

Look in the mirror. Smile. Tell yourself words you really need to hear.

11

1. Today, take extra good care of yourself.
2. Take a long shower/bath, brush your teeth, put on your favorite clothes, do your hair/makeup, dab on some perfume/cologne.
3. Go do something nice for yourself, something you'll enjoy. (Really important: pick something that *you*, not someone else, would like to do.)
4. Buy a little (or big) something you'd like to have that'll bring you joy.
5. Repeat often.

Look in the mirror. Smile. Tell yourself words you really need to hear.

12

1. Today, be present.
2. Don't look backward & dredge up your history.
3. Don't look forward into an unknown future.
4. If you do, *gently* remind yourself to stay in the present moment.
5. Then find something in the present moment that brings you joy.
6. Repeat often.
7. Reminder: add one more positive self-attribute to your list from Day 4.

Look in the mirror. Smile. Tell yourself words you really need to hear.

13

1. Today, be grateful.
2. Write a list of at least five things (big or small) that you're grateful for.
3. Read through that list.
4. Be reminded that there are *always* good things in your life (even if you have to do a little digging to find them).
5. Repeat often.
6. Know this: gratitude is an easy thing to do that will encourage you & change your entire outlook for the better as long as you practice it.

Look in the mirror. Smile. Tell yourself words you really need to hear.

14

1. Today, forgive yourself for all the mistakes you'll make today & for all the mistakes you've already made in the past.
2. Be kind & patient with yourself.
3. Write a list of mistakes that you're hanging on to. Then write what you can learn from each mistake so you can more intelligently try again. Now let those mistakes go & begin again.
4. Know this: the only difference between people who succeed & people who fail is the former group doesn't let their mistakes derail them.

Look in the mirror. Smile. Tell yourself words you really need to hear.

15

1. Today, stop comparing.
2. Know this: comparison truly is an act of self-abuse.
3. So don't compare yourself to anyone else, not about anything, for the whole day. If you find yourself comparing, *gently* remind yourself to stop.
4. Read through the growing list you started on Day 4.
5. Now add five more things that are fabulous about you & be reminded of all the things you have to offer.

Look in the mirror. Smile. Tell yourself words you really need to hear.

16

1. Today, go do something you enjoy.
2. Get away from whatever's got you discouraged & get out of your own head for a while.
3. Have fun. Play. Relax.
4. Come back rejuvenated & refreshed.
5. Repeat often.
6. Reminder: add one more positive self-attribute to your list from Day 4.

Look in the mirror. Smile. Tell yourself words you really need to hear.

17

1. Today, ignore everyone's opinion (good or bad) of you.
2. Know this: the only opinion of you that truly matters is your own.
3. So hold on to your peace & open yourself up to abundance by focusing on what's amazing about you.
4. Take another look at your growing list from Day 4.
5. Add five more things that are phenomenal about you. Now ignore everyone else's opinion of you & base your opinion of yourself on what you find on that list.

Look in the mirror. Smile. Tell yourself words you really need to hear.

18

1. Today, make a bucket list.
2. Write at least ten things *you* want to do/have/be/experience while you're still around.
3. Be brave. Pick one & go do it. Or if it takes some planning, start planning today & write a date when you'll be finished then circle that date on your calendar. Be honorable & keep your word to yourself.
4. Work your way down that list, finishing one thing then the next then the next. After you check everything off, make a new list.

Look in the mirror. Smile. Tell yourself words you really need to hear.

19

1. Today, come alive.
2. Write the answers to these: *What do I love to do &/or what lights a spark in me? What activities make me feel the most alive? What are my gifts & talents & passions (things that I love & enjoy)?*
3. Know this: a gift/talent/passion is *anything* that brings you joy & makes you feel alive (whether you receive material gain from it or not).
4. Go *do* one of those activities/gifts/talents/passions today & enjoy yourself.

Look in the mirror. Smile. Tell yourself words you really need to hear.

20

1. Today, reorganize your priorities.
2. Take a look at your answers from Day 19. Then take a look at your typical day/week.
3. Write the answers to these: *If I'm not doing what I most love to do, what needs to change so I can start? If I am doing it, what needs to change so I can do more of it?*
4. Rearrange your schedule today (oh, yes you can!) so you can find some time to nourish yourself by doing more of what you love to do.

Look in the mirror. Smile. Tell yourself words you really need to hear.

21

1. Today, feel the music.
2. Put on your favorite song/station/musician. Crank up the volume.
3. Sing along. Loudly. Off-key if that's the best you can do. Embarrass your spouse/friends/kids. Who cares? This is about you. Just sing.
4. Dance. Shake what your mama gave you. Vigorously. Embarrass your spouse/friends/kids. Who cares? This is about you. Just dance.
5. Reminder: add one more positive self-attribute to your list from Day 4.

Look in the mirror. Smile. Tell yourself words you really need to hear.

22

1. Today, be adventurous.
2. Write a list of at least five places *you* would really like to go, preferably somewhere new.
3. Now pick one & go there & take in the sights along the way.
4. Have fun!
5. Get yourself a souvenir to remind you that you're worth spending time, energy, & money on.
6. Reminder: add one more positive self-attribute to your list from Day 4.

Look in the mirror. Smile. Tell yourself words you really need to hear.

23

1. Today, learn something new.
2. Write a list of at least five things *you* would love to know how to do.
3. Now pick one & take the time to read a book, take a class, hire a private instructor, etcetera to learn how to do it.
4. Know this: You are worth spending the time, energy, & money on yourself to better yourself & bring yourself fulfillment.
5. Reminder: add one more positive self-attribute to your list from Day 4.

Look in the mirror. Smile. Tell yourself words you really need to hear.

24

1. Today, be generous.
2. Do something kind (big or small) for somebody else with the sole motivation of simply lending a helping hand.
3. Give some of your time/money/brawn/knowledge/etcetera to a cause/person who needs it.
4. Take note of how much the world really does need your help to make it a better place.
5. Reminder: add one more positive self-attribute to your list from Day 4.

Look in the mirror. Smile. Tell yourself words you really need to hear.

25

1. Today, slow down.
2. Go to the space you created on Day 10. Take ten deep breaths (in through your nose, hold three seconds, then let it out your mouth).
3. Now go outside. Tip your face up to the sky. Or sit under a tree. Or go for a long walk. Or relax in a hammock. Or pick some wildflowers. Or whatever will help you calm down & center yourself.
4. Take in nature & be reminded that it's a big world & you're part of it, not at odds with it.

Look in the mirror. Smile. Tell yourself words you really need to hear.

26

1. Today, enjoy someone's company.
2. Go hang out with a person/pet you love or at least like a whole lot.
3. Do something that you'll both enjoy.
4. Stay in the moment (so let go of all your worries & to-do lists while you're together).
5. Belly laugh at least once.
6. Have a great time!
7. Repeat often.

Look in the mirror. Smile. Tell yourself words you really need to hear.

27

1. Today, find the gift(s) in whatever you're going through.
2. Know this: the gift (& it really is a gift, you'll come to find out) is what you can learn from the situation.
3. The lesson may be the size of a pinprick & heavily camouflaged & take some serious excavating to find. But look until you find it.
4. Write down any & all gift(s) that you find.
5. Now take those gifts to heart & learn from them so that you can more intelligently move on &/or begin again.

Look in the mirror. Smile. Tell yourself words you really need to hear.

28

1. Today, change the story you're telling yourself about: your past, your present, yourself, your ability to succeed, & the list goes on.
2. Know this: you *always* have the option to edit the voice in your head.
3. So write a list of any events/mistakes that are holding you back &/or you are beating yourself up over.
4. Now consider this: what if those events/mistakes happened to teach you how strong/tenacious/courageous/forgiving/etcetera you are?
5. Choose to see them in a different light & write a new story about each.

Look in the mirror. Smile. Tell yourself words you really need to hear.

29

1. Today, free yourself by being yourself.
2. No need to impress or prove or pretend to be anybody you are not.
3. Take a deep breath in through your nose, hold for three seconds, let it out your mouth. Let your shoulders relax. Feel your whole body relax.
4. Now read through the lists from Day 4 & Day 19. That's who you are & what you love. And that is enough. You are enough.
5. Say this aloud: *I am enough right now, as-is.*
6. Repeat often.

Look in the mirror. Smile. Tell yourself words you really need to hear.

30

1. Today, celebrate!
2. Be proud of yourself for how far you've come.
3. Write down your successes & victories (big or small).
4. Do something nice for yourself (like a prize for a job well done).
5. Go & enjoy your life!

Look in the mirror. Smile. Tell yourself words you really need to hear.

ABOUT THE AUTHOR!

This book was born out of Shelli Johnson's own struggle with discouragement. She wanted and needed to heal herself. She wanted and needed practical and easy steps she could take to encourage herself. So she simply wrote the book she needed to read. Every day, she does her best to cut herself some slack & practice progress, not perfection.

Shelli's also an award-winning journalist (sports reporting), novelist (grand prize winner), and blogger (shellijohnson.com/blog). She's a truck owner, horse rider, photographer, yoga enthusiast, and slow-cooker fan (shellijohnson.com/recipes). Find out more at: shellijohnson.com/about

Find out about Shelli's other books at:
shellijohnson.com/books

GET YOUR FREE STUFF!

Visit: shellijohnson.com/signup
Opt-in for the newsletter to keep in touch.
Get a free bookmark to color.

ACKNOWLEDGMENTS!

My sincere thanks to people who make my days brighter:
Rollin Johnson
Heather Porazzo

Disclosures and Disclaimers

This book is published in print format. All trademarks and service marks are the properties of their respective owners. All references to these properties are made solely for editorial purposes. Except for marks actually owned by the Author or the Publisher, no commercial claims are made to their use, and neither the Author nor the Publisher is affiliated with such marks in any way.

Unless otherwise expressly noted, none of the individuals or business entities mentioned herein has endorsed the contents of this book.

Limits of Liability & Disclaimers of Warranties

Because this book is a general educational information product, it is not a substitute for professional advice on the topics discussed in it.

The materials in this book are provided "as is" and without warranties of any kind either express or implied. The Author and the Publisher disclaim all warranties, express or implied, including, but not limited to, implied warranties of merchantability and fitness for a particular purpose. The Author and the Publisher do not warrant that defects will be corrected. The Author does not warrant or make any representations regarding the use or the results of the use of the materials in this book in terms of their correctness, accuracy, reliability, or otherwise. Applicable law may not allow the exclusion of implied warranties, so the above exclusion may not apply to you.

Under no circumstances, including, but not limited to, negligence, shall the Author or the Publisher be liable for any special or consequential damages that result from the use of, or the inability to use this book, even if the Author, the Publisher, or an authorized representative has been advised of the possibility of such damages. Applicable law may not allow the limitation or exclusion of liability or incidental or consequential damages, so the above limitation or exclusion may not apply to you. In no event shall the Author or Publisher total liability to you for all damages, losses, and causes of action (whether in contract, tort, including but not limited to, negligence or otherwise) exceed the amount paid by you, if any, for this book.

You agree to hold the Author and the Publisher of this book, principals, agents, affiliates, and employees harmless from any and all liability for all claims for damages due to injuries, including attorney fees and costs, incurred by you or caused to third parties by you, arising out of the products, services, and activities discussed in this book, excepting only claims for gross negligence or intentional tort.

You agree that any and all claims for gross negligence or intentional tort shall be settled solely by confidential binding arbitration per the American Arbitration Association's commercial arbitration rules. Your claim cannot be aggregated with third party claims. All arbitration must occur in the municipality where the Author's principal place of business is located. Arbitration fees and costs shall be split equally, and you are solely responsible for your own lawyer fees.

Facts and information are believed to be accurate at the time they were placed in this book. All data provided in this book is to be used for information purposes only. The information contained within is not intended to provide specific legal, financial, tax, physical or mental health advice, or any other advice whatsoever, for any individual or company and should not be relied upon in that regard. The services described are only offered in jurisdictions where they may be legally offered. Information provided is not all-inclusive, and is limited to information that is made available and such information should not be relied upon as all-inclusive or accurate.

For more information about this policy, please contact the Author at the website address listed in the Copyright Notice at the front of this book.

IF YOU DO NOT AGREE WITH THESE TERMS AND EXPRESS CONDITIONS, DO NOT READ THIS BOOK. YOUR USE OF THIS BOOK, INCLUDING PRODUCTS, SERVICES, AND ANY PARTICIPATION IN ACTIVITIES MENTIONED IN THIS BOOK, MEAN THAT YOU ARE AGREEING TO BE LEGALLY BOUND BY THESE TERMS.

Affiliate Compensation & Material Connections Disclosure

This book may contain references to websites and information created and maintained by other individuals and organizations. The Author and the Publisher do not control or guarantee the accuracy, completeness, relevance, or timeliness of any information or privacy policies posted on these websites.

You should assume that all references to products and services in this book are made because material connections exist between the Author or Publisher and the providers of the mentioned products and services ("Provider"). You should also assume that all website links within this book are affiliate links for (a) the Author, (b) the Publisher, or (c) someone else who is an affiliate for the mentioned products and services (individually and collectively, the "Affiliate").

The Affiliate recommends products and services in this book based in part on a good faith belief that the purchase of such products or services will help readers in general.

The Affiliate has this good faith belief because (a) the Affiliate has tried the product or service mentioned prior to recommending it or (b) the Affiliate has researched the reputation of the Provider and has made the decision to recommend the Provider's products or services based on the Provider's history of providing these or other products or services.

The representations made by the Affiliate about products and services reflect the Affiliate's honest opinion based upon the facts known to the Affiliate at the time this book was published.

Because there is a material connection between the Affiliate and Providers of products or services mentioned in this book, you should always assume that the Affiliate may be biased because of the Affiliate's relationship with a Provider and/or because the Affiliate has received or will receive something of value from a Provider.

Perform your own due diligence before purchasing a product or service mentioned in this book.

The type of compensation received by the Affiliate may vary. In some instances, the Affiliate may receive complimentary products (such as a review copy), services, or money from a Provider prior to mentioning the Provider's products or services in this book.

In addition, the Affiliate may receive a monetary commission or non-monetary compensation when you take action by using a website link within in this book. This includes, but is not limited to, when you purchase a product or service from a Provider after going to a website link contained in this book.

Health Disclaimers

As an express condition to reading to this book, you understand and agree to the following terms.

This book is a general educational health-related information product. This book does not contain medical advice.

The book's content is not a substitute for direct, personal, professional medical care and diagnosis. None of the exercises or treatments (including products and services) mentioned in this book should be performed or otherwise used without prior approval from your physician or other qualified professional health care provider.

There may be risks associated with participating in activities or using products and services mentioned in this book for people in poor health or with pre-existing physical or mental health conditions.

Because these risks exist, you will not use such products or participate in such activities if you are in poor health or have a pre-existing mental or physical condition. If you choose to participate in these risks, you do so of your own free will and accord, knowingly and voluntarily assuming all risks associated with such activities.

Earnings & Income Disclaimers
No Earnings Projections, Promises or Representations

For purposes of these disclaimers, the term "Author" refers individually and collectively to the author of this book and to the affiliate (if any) whose affiliate hyperlinks are referenced in this book.

You recognize and agree that the Author and the Publisher have made no implications, warranties, promises, suggestions, projections, representations or guarantees whatsoever to you about future prospects or earnings, or that you will earn any money, with respect to your purchase of this book, and that the Author and the Publisher have not authorized any such projection, promise, or representation by others.

Any earnings or income statements, or any earnings or income examples, are only estimates of what you might earn. There is no assurance you will do as well as stated in any examples. If you rely upon any figures provided, you must accept the entire risk of not doing as well as the information provided. This applies whether the earnings or income examples are monetary in nature or pertain to advertising credits which may be earned (whether such credits are convertible to cash or not).

There is no assurance that any prior successes or past results as to earnings or income (whether monetary or advertising credits, whether convertible to cash or not) will apply, nor can any prior successes be used, as an indication of your future success or results from any of the information, content, or strategies. Any and all claims or representations as to income or earnings (whether monetary or advertising credits, whether convertible to cash or not) are not to be considered as "average earnings".

Testimonials & Examples

Testimonials and examples in this book are exceptional results, do not reflect the typical purchaser's experience, do not apply to the average person and are not intended to represent or guarantee that anyone will achieve the same or similar results. Where specific income or earnings (whether monetary or advertising credits, whether convertible to cash or not), figures are used and attributed to a specific individual or business, that individual or business has earned that amount. There is no assurance that you will do as well using the same information or strategies. If you rely on the specific income or earnings figures used, you must accept all the risk of not doing as well. The described experiences are atypical. Your financial results are likely to differ from those described in the testimonials.

The Economy

The economy, where you do business, on a national and even worldwide scale, creates additional uncertainty and economic risk. An economic recession or depression might negatively affect your results.

Your Success or Lack of It

Your success in using the information or strategies provided in this book depends on a variety of factors. The Author and the Publisher have no way of knowing how well you will do because they do not know you, your background, your work ethic, your dedication, your motivation, your desire, or your business skills or practices. Therefore, neither the Author nor the Publisher guarantees or implies that you will get rich, that you will do as well, or that you will have any earnings (whether monetary or advertising credits, whether convertible to cash or not), at all.

Businesses and earnings derived therefrom involve unknown risks and are not suitable for everyone. You may not rely on any information presented in this book or otherwise provided by the Author or the Publisher, unless you do so with the knowledge and understanding that you can experience significant losses (including, but not limited to, the loss of any monies paid to purchase this book and/or any monies spent setting up, operating, and/or marketing your business activities, and further, that you may have no earnings at all (whether monetary or advertising credits, whether convertible to cash or not).

Forward-Looking Statements

Materials in this book may contain information that includes or is based upon forward-looking statements within the meaning of the Securities Litigation Reform Act of 1995. Forward-looking statements give the Author's expectations or forecasts of future events. You can identify these statements by the fact that they do not relate strictly to historical or current facts. They use words such as "anticipate," "estimate," "expect," "project," "intend," "plan," "believe," and other words and terms of similar meaning in connection with a description of potential earnings or financial performance.

Any and all forward looking statements here or on any materials in this book are intended to express an opinion of earnings potential. Many factors will be important in determining your actual results and no guarantees are made that you will achieve results similar to the Author or anybody else. In fact, no guarantees are made that you will achieve any results from applying the Author's ideas, strategies, and tactics found in this book.

Purchase Price

Although the Publisher believes the price is fair for the value that you receive, you understand and agree that the purchase price for this book has been arbitrarily set by the Publisher or the vendor who sold you this book. This price bears no relationship to objective standards.

Due Diligence

You are advised to do your own due diligence when it comes to making any decisions. Use caution and seek the advice of qualified professionals before acting upon the contents of this book or any other information. You shall not consider any examples, documents, or other content in this book or otherwise provided by the Author or Publisher to be the equivalent of professional advice.

The Author and the Publisher assume no responsibility for any losses or damages resulting from your use of any link, information, or opportunity contained in this book or within any other information disclosed by the Author or the Publisher in any form whatsoever.

YOU SHOULD ALWAYS CONDUCT YOUR OWN INVESTIGATION (PERFORM DUE DILIGENCE) BEFORE BUYING PRODUCTS OR SERVICES FROM ANYONE. THIS INCLUDES PRODUCTS AND SERVICES SOLD VIA WEBSITE LINKS REFERENCED IN THIS BOOK.

www.ingramcontent.com/pod-product-compliance
Lightning Source LLC
Chambersburg PA
CBHW060515300426
44112CB00017B/2681